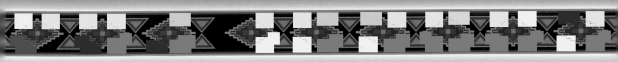

DREAM CATCHING

TABLE OF CONTENTS

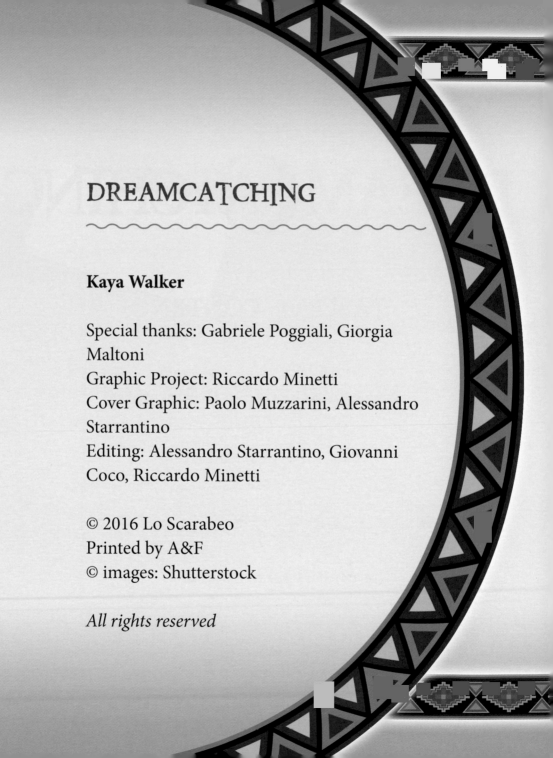

DREAMCATCHING

Kaya Walker

Special thanks: Gabriele Poggiali, Giorgia Maltoni
Graphic Project: Riccardo Minetti
Cover Graphic: Paolo Muzzarini, Alessandro Starrantino
Editing: Alessandro Starrantino, Giovanni Coco, Riccardo Minetti

INTRODUCTION

This little booklet provides a few general ideas about dreamcatchers. Most importantly, as will be discussed later, this introduction to dreamcatchers does not pretend to be a treatise on Native American dreamcatcher traditions and practices. It is a Western adaptation of a spiritual tool. In these pages you will learn about ways you can use a dreamcatcher to make your life healthier and more peaceful. We'll talk about the various elements of dreamcatchers, what they symbolize, and how to personalize dreamcatchers to suit specific needs. Dreamcatchers are well known for helping with dream work and we will discuss that in more detail in Part 3. Finally, you'll learn ways—that may surprise you—that a dreamcatcher can not only help with dreams but also change the spiritual environment of the area in which it is placed.

PART 1.

INTRODUCTION TO DREAMCATCHERS

Dreamcatchers have caught not only innumerable "bad" dreams but also the attention of many non-Native Americans. Their beauty and their promise of peace and happiness draw us toward them even though we don't fully understand what they are, everything they are capable of, and the intricacies of their design. This little book hopes to share some ideas so that more can appreciate their beauty and benefit from their gifts.

POPULARITY

The New Age movement, the cross-cultural sharing of spiritual practices, and easy global communication encourages us all to be our best selves, to live our best lives, and to do it all in an easy and peaceful manner. We assume that success is our birthright and that if we do not achieve professional, romantic, domestic, and creative goals every week, then we simply aren't trying hard enough. But don't forget to keep your Zen cool! Maybe you just need (another) 30-Day Spiritual Cleansing Boot Camp.

With all this striving, all these expectations, and all the tools and techniques available to us, we have to achieve certain levels of personal growth at exponential rates. Honestly, it can be exhausting. It is easy to think "just for one week, it'd be nice not have a revelation that requires an overhaul of some aspect

WE UNDERSTAND
THAT THE
DREAMCATCHER
IS A SPIRITUAL AID
THAT DOES NOT
REQUIRE MUCH EFFORT
OR KNOWLEDGE
ON OUR PART.

of my life!" When can we slow down or take a break? It's like we want a holiday from the hard work of becoming spiritually mature human beings (to say nothing of also trying to become physically healthy, mentally agile, and emotionally stable at the same time).

This is probably one reason why dreamcatchers are so popular. Most of us have seen them in gift shops, in museums or galleries, in metaphysical shops. Even though dreamcatchers originated in Native American cultures, they have become part of the larger popular culture of the world. While many of us don't know all the interesting details about dreamcatchers (this book will help with that!), we do have a general idea of what they are and how they work. We understand (or assume) that the dreamcatcher is a spiritual aid that does not require much effort or knowledge on our part. We can just hang it up somewhere and it works. In some ways this is quite true.

TO USE A
DREAMCACTHER,
WE DON'T HAVE TO
TAKE ANY ACTION
OR MAKE ANY
CONSCIOUS
EFFORTS.

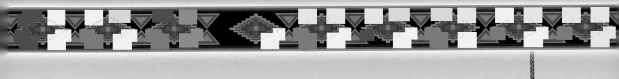

Another reason they may be so popular is the opposite end of the spectrum. We know we have a spiritual self, but instead of working very hard at trying to evolve it, we are too nervous or scared to even approach attending to the spirit. We may be too invested in our material lives or we be afraid of the knowledge that comes with spiritual awareness. We know, at some level, if we start looking at our spiritual needs, we would have to change the way we live our lives. For those of us in this situation, a dreamcatcher is perfect. It is not scary at all. It is cute and decorative. We can even pretend that it is art and not a spiritual aid. We don't have to take any action or make any conscious efforts. We don't even have to believe it is doing anything much for it to make us feel better. We might even think of it as a spiritual version of the tree-shaped car freshener: it just makes the atmosphere more pleasant.

PURPOSE

When we decide to acquire a dreamcatcher, whether it is an intentional seeking or an impulse purchase, we are, at least on some level, acknowledging our spiritual or invisible life and the space it inhabits. It also means that either we recognize the need for spiritual maintenance or that we are aware of a spiritual or energetic need that is not being satisfied or of an imbalance. For most of us, the acquisition of a dreamcatcher is not something that is researched and analyzed. Usually we see one that catches our fancy and don't think twice before taking it home and hanging it up. The spiritual need or imbalance likely never entered our minds; instead, our subconscious helped guide us toward an experience that was gentle enough for our conscious minds not to freak out about.

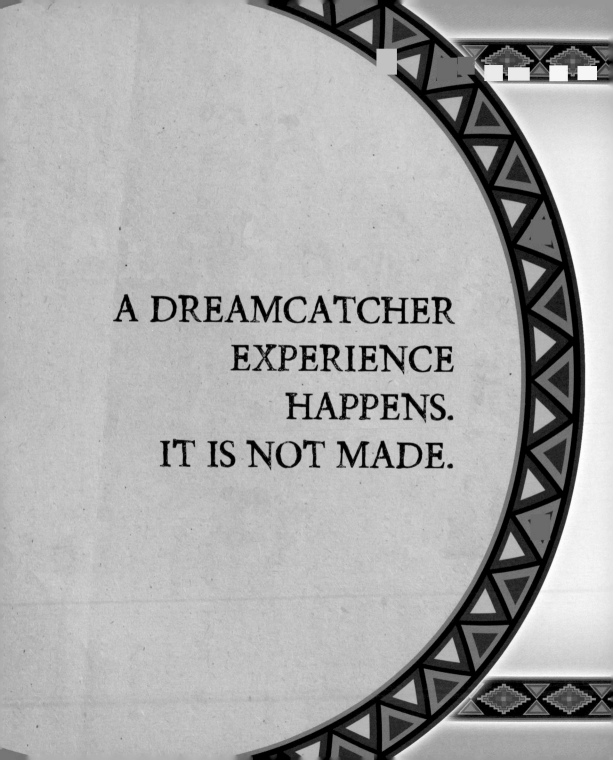

A DREAMCATCHER
EXPERIENCE
HAPPENS.
IT IS NOT MADE.

This is perfectly normal and totally okay. So many times a dreamcatcher choice should not be a rational, analytical activity. A dreamcatcher experience happens; it is not made. This is why the answer to the question "How long does a dreamcatcher work" is "until it is no longer needed."

When you hang a dreamcatcher, you probably, like most of us, imagine that the delicate strands making the web-like interior "catch" bad dreams that try to inhabit our sleep while the hole in the middle lets the good dreams fill our sleeping minds. This is true, but it is also more than that. By hanging a dreamcatcher, you begin a journey that has no destination. It is more like a stroll around the spiritual landscape rather than a purposeful stride toward a spiritual goal. The key is to let it happen. This is easier to do when you're not being overly conscious or analytical, so random dreamcatcher acquisition can be a really

15

beneficial thing and even work better than a more deliberate approach.

Dreams are expressions of our subconscious. We tend to romanticize the subconscious, thinking that it is filled with only good or necessary information, insights, and ideas that would surely help us if only we could access them. But the subconscious holds a lot of more than just precious and mind-blowing insights. It is the depository of everything that the conscious mind either cannot handle or is completely obsessed with. If you have an anxiety dream about trying to leave the house for an important appointment but cannot find your wallet or car keys the night before a job interview, that isn't really revelatory. It is the subconscious mind trying to help alleviate the stress of the conscious mind. The effort is wasted, though, as it does not help at all, but instead makes for a poor night's sleep. It isn't a necessary dream. It isn't a particular-

ly helpful dream. Therefore the idea of catching what we would call bad dreams is very useful, especially during periods of extreme stress.

When you place your dreamcatcher over your bed (or wherever you sleep), it will block bad dreams by tangling them up in the threads that create the web. They stay there, stuck to the web threads, until morning, when the sun (also symbolic of our consciousness) causes them to dissolve and evaporate into nothingness. Your good dreams pass back and forth through the hole, from your sleeping mind to the spirit realm, thus creating a connection. Once the connection is formed, good dreams are more easily drawn to your mind.

Dreamcatchers do not only work for your personal dreams at night. Dreamcatchers also affect the general area around them, which is why some people hang them in other parts

DREAMCATCHERS
ACT AS A CONNECTION
BETWEEN EARTH AND
HEAVEN, THE MATERIAL
AND THE SPIRITUAL,
BELOW AND ABOVE.

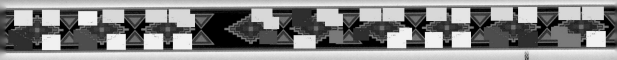

of the house, in addition to sleeping areas. They act as a connection between earth and heaven, the material and the spiritual, below and above. In fact, this role of connector is really the dreamcatcher's most important; it is the essential nature of a dreamcatcher. Just as they help sort out our dreams, separating the good from the bad and encouraging more good, they also purify the energy of a home or space and encourage the flow of pure and beneficial energy. They can protect and comfort children (or anyone in need), absorb anger, and facilitate communication, and more. Although not all dreamcatchers have the same purpose…or rather dreamcatchers are designed to specialize in certain functions. This is part of the interesting detail you find in the pages that follow.

APPROPRIATION

As mentioned above, dreamcatchers come to us from Native American practices. Because we live in a more interconnected world than ever before, spiritual (as well as other types of) practices are being shared and taught to wider audiences. This sharing of ideas enriches everyone and through this sharing, we evolve and create something new. There is much concern about cultural appropriation and rightly so; it is a complex issue that goes beyond who is using a particular tool or practice. So many of us have crafted unique spiritual paths using ideas and practices we've learned along the way and not ones that are necessarily associated with the culture we were born and raised in. This is a good thing because we are learning, as humans, that just because we were born into a certain culture (or gendered body) doesn't mean that it is the right one for us.

THERE IS
THE QUESTION
OF RESPECT
AND HONOR,
AND GRATITUDE

Also, one wonders to what extent Spirit cares about accidents of birth limiting how one connects with and worships the Divine. Culture, ethnicity, national memory… these are all part of us but they do not dictate the whole of who we are and do not take from us the free will to worship and connect in whatever way feels authentic to our souls.

And yet, there is the question of respect and honor… and gratitude. People must decide for themselves whether they will stick strictly to the practices of their birth culture or will integrate ideas from other cultures. If you do integrate other ideas, tools, and practices, such as using a dreamcatcher, do so with intelligence, respect, honor, and gratitude. Be aware that any practice adapted from another culture will be changed in the transfer. For example, many non-Hindus (or non-Buddhists or non-Jainists) today practice yoga with the knowledge that what they do is very

different from how a Hindu would practice, however, they still benefit from the practice. So the dream catching practice presented here is not what it means to use a dreamcatcher as a Native American, but rather what it means to adapt dreamcatchers to a modern, pluralistic, global spiritual generation.

We honor and thank the Spirits that guided the Native Americans in the practice of dream catching. We are grateful that we live in a world where an even wider audience can learn about dreamcatchers and can adapt them to almost any sort of personal practice.

However, this is not the only possible way to look at the issue. This article provides a very pertinent argument against cultural appropriation: *http://www.thepeoplespaths.net/articles/formlife.htm*

27

PART 2.

PURPOSE AND DESIGN

Most of us think of dreamcatchers as talismans that take away bad dreams and we think that they are a circular frame with threads and beads and feathers arranged in a decorative manner. These ideas are true, but they are not the whole or only truth. This section will explore the purposes of these elements a little further and will explain some of the interesting aspects of their design. The more you know about any tool you use, the more effectively you can use it. Also, dreamcatchers are so much more intricate and magical than is commonly believed, it is important to spread the word.

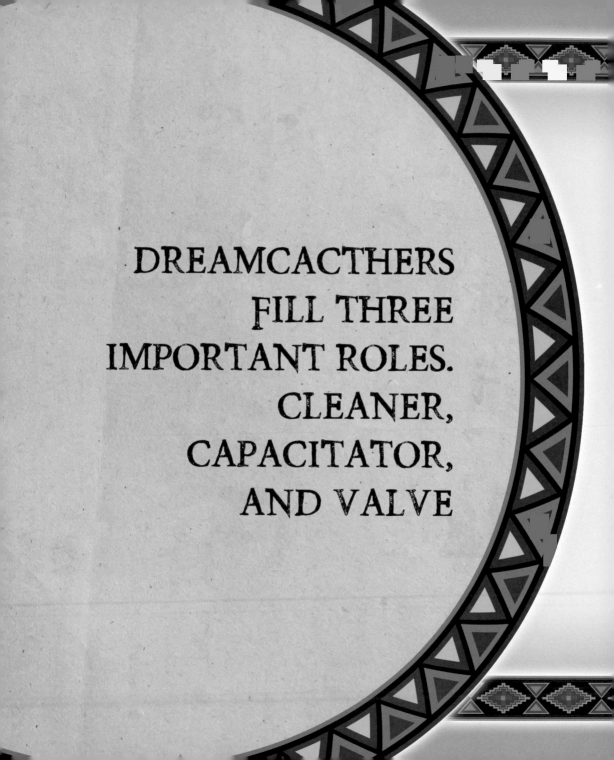

DREAMCACTHERS
FILL THREE
IMPORTANT ROLES.
CLEANER,
CAPACITATOR,
AND VALVE

WHAT DO DREAMCATCHERS DO?

Dreamcatchers do more than just "catch" bad dreams. As discussed earlier, they also draw or attract good dreams. So they are more than a filtration system. They are a connection between the material and the spiritual realms. What functions do they perform in their role of connector? There are three important ones: cleaner, capacitator, and valve. We mentioned the role of cleaner earlier. Dreamcatchers acting as a cleaner are the closest to being a filter. A filter separates things and likewise, a dreamcatcher separates good and bad energy, thereby helping cleanse the energy in an area. As a capacitator, a dreamcatcher stores or holds energy. As a valve, a dreamcatcher controls the flow of energy between the material and spiritual realms. This sounds pretty abstract. The easiest way to explain and understand these functions is through exploring the design theory of dreamcatchers.

31

HOW DO DREAMCATCHERS WORK?

Here are the basic components and what they do. Dreamcatchers should be hung above head level. If hung in a bedroom or by a sleeping area, head level can be considered where the head is when sleeping. If hung in another area to help cleanse and energize the environment, then "head level" will be higher.

- Energy flows from below, upward toward the dreamcatcher.
- The feathers guide the energy.
- The thread blocks the bad energy.
- The stones or beads power or support the work of the thread.
- The circular design creates greater harmony.

33

SIZE MATTERS

I don't mean the size of the dreamcatcher, but rather the size of the center hole and the spaces in the webbing. These are determined by the purpose of the dreamcatcher. Larger holes mean a larger connection or valve opening, allowing energy to flow more freely. The smaller the holes, the more energy is gathered and altered by the dreamcatcher. If you hang a dreamcatcher with the intent to promote communication with the spirit world, then you would want a wider net with a larger center hole. For cleansing, protection, or gathering energy, a tighter web with a smaller hole would serve your purposes better.

ROUGH AND SMOOTH THREAD

Smooth or regular thread is the most commonly used and perfectly fine for most purposes. Garden-variety bad dreams are not only confusing but also confused, so they are more easily distracted and caught by the webbing. However, for deeper personal shadow work, the thought patterns are generally older and more evolved. They are stronger, more persistent, and more determined to stay alive. Therefore using rougher or courser thread is usually employed for dreamcatchers intended for heavy-duty purposes.

BALANCED AND SPIRAL WEB DESIGN

There are different weaving designs for the webbing. A balanced pattern is more stable, providing a nice, easy flow of energy. It takes what comes its way and it gives in measured and composed amounts. A spiral pattern is more active. It actively attracts energy and moves energy back and forth with more force.

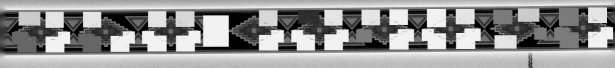

DOUBLE CIRCLE

All dreamcatchers have a large circle defining the outside circumference (usually made of wood), which represents the earth. Some dreamcatchers have a second wooden circle, an inner circle in the center, that represents heaven. In other dreamcatchers, the inner circle is created by the weaving pattern of the thread. Dreamcatchers with a double circle have an extra powerful boost, which is not always necessary or desired. Your intended use will determine which is best for your purposes.

COLOR

Color is a very powerful and evocative symbol for humans. Different systems or beliefs often share similar interpretations for color, although sometimes there are variations. Here are some of the most common color associations used in dreamcatcher creation.

- **White:** Air and wind. Used to encourage the free flowing of thoughts and easy communication.
- **Black:** Earth and the physical world. Used to beckon spiritual energy to earth.
- **Brown:** The horizon line, where the earth meets the sky. Used to increase vision and connection.
- **Yellow:** Fire and spirituality. Used to invite shamanic experience and spiritual awareness.
- **Red:** Fire, passion, and deep, innate drives. Used to connect with the most primal kind of wisdom.

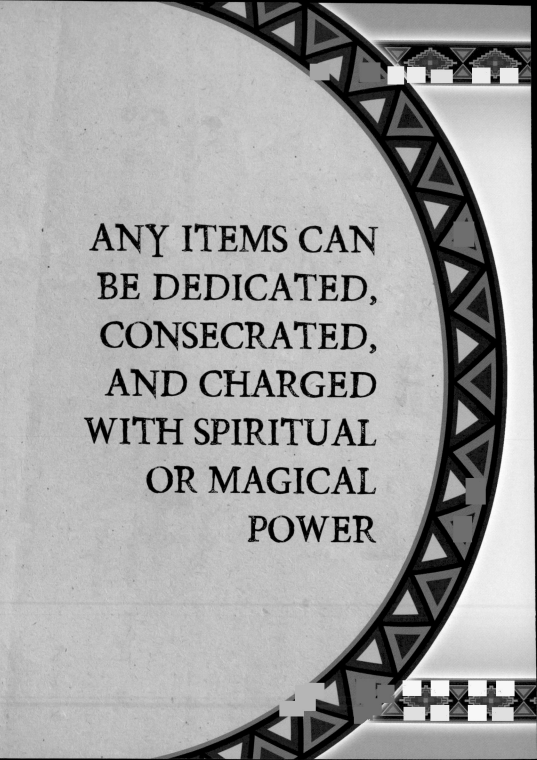

ANY ITEMS CAN
BE DEDICATED,
CONSECRATED,
AND CHARGED
WITH SPIRITUAL
OR MAGICAL
POWER

FEATHERS

While it may seem romantic and "authen-tic" to include eagle feathers, it is illegal to gather or possess raptor feathers except for Native Americans using them in traditional practices. As mentioned earlier, the trans-lating a practice from one culture to anoth-er will necessarily change that practice, in both mundane and spiritual ways. Please do not attempt to obtain eagle or other raptor feathers.

Other feathers are available to use and you are encouraged to work with materi-als that are legal and ethical in your area. While there is energy in "real" items (crys-tals, plants, feathers, etc.), we also know that intent is nearly as important and that any items can be dedicated, consecrat-ed, and charged with spiritual or magical power.

Feathers are the guides in a dreamcatcher. They are associated with the element of Air and are the conduits that attract and draw the energy into and through the dreamcatcher. By carefully selecting the colors (both the actual colors and the relationship to the colors used in the thread and beads), you can design your dreamcatcher so that it can best achieve what you want.

Using legally and ethically obtained feathers, we can employ the symbolic usage described here:

- **Single color stacked:** Feathers of the same or similar color, often the same as the colors used in the thread and beads, and of a similar size. This is commonly used when you wish to affect a single type of energy or have a single, focused intent.

47

- **Double color stacked:** There are two variations of this technique.

1. Feathers of the same or similar color but different from the thread and beads. Used to affect different specific energies or, if the colors cover a broad spectrum, used to affect the general energy of a space.

2. Feathers that are of different colors but similar to the ones used in the beads and thread and affixed in different rows indicate a desire to transform energy.

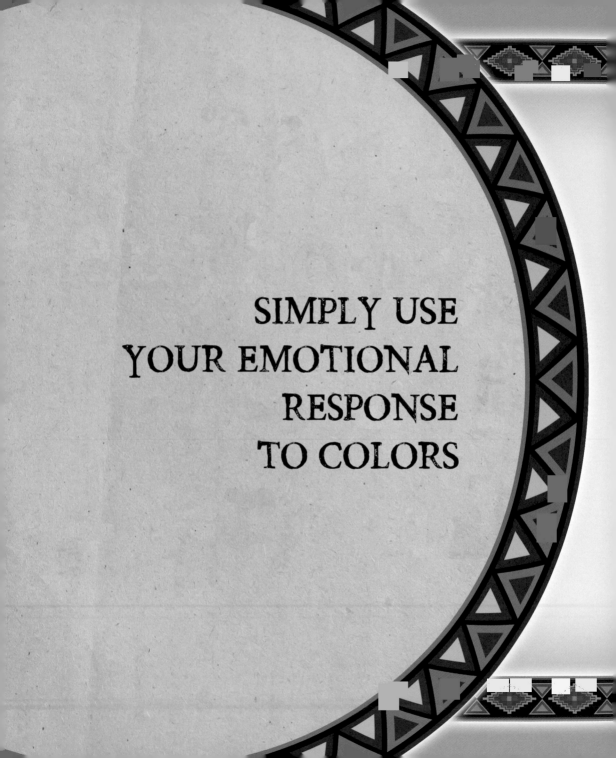

SIMPLY USE
YOUR EMOTIONAL
RESPONSE
TO COLORS

BEADS

As mentioned earlier, beads power up the thread that the web is made of. The type of beads used will affect the thread's purpose. Also, the number of beads and their place-ment will also shape the effects that the dreamcatcher will have on the environment.

The beads used in dreamcatchers are usually made of stone or crystal. If you have knowl-edge of or access to a good crystal dictionary, you can select very specific beads that will support your intent. If not, you can rely on using your knowledge of color symbolism (or, if you have none, simply use your emo-tional response to colors) to select which bead or beads would be best.

Below are guidelines for the number of beads and placement.

Single bead

When a single bead is used, generally it is placed in the center of the dreamcatcher. The energy collected by thread is gathered around the bead and passes through it becoming enhanced, charged, cleansed, or transformed depending on the intent and design of the dreamcatcher.

Random beads

Randomly placed beads, particularly an odd number of them, alters the symmetry of the dreamcatcher. This is very useful if you want to break up the stagnation in an environment.

Balance

By placing an even number of beads in a balanced and symmetrical manner, the symmetry and balance of the dreamcatcher is enhanced. Stability and harmony are strengthened because the flow of energy in and out is regulated.

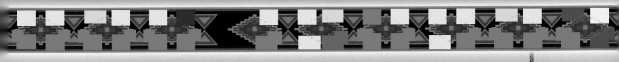

Circle or thread

Beads can be placed on the circle(s) or on the thread.

When placed on the outer circle, which represents the earth, the energy connected to the material plane is strengthened. When placed on the inner circle (if the dreamcatcher has one, of course), the energy associated with heaven or spirit is intensified.

When the beads are placed on the thread, either in the webbing or near the feathers, they fortify the web and strongly impart the bead's energy to the energy passing through the dreamcatcher.

55

SELECTING
A DREAMCATCHER

Your first instinct might be to pick one that you think is pretty or attractive or perhaps one the matches the colors of the room you want to hang it in. As mentioned before, that can work very well, but now that you know more about how dreamcatchers work, you can choose one that will best achieve the goal you desire. So really the first step is figuring out what you need it to accomplish.

Once you know that, you can think about the best "medicine" or approach to accomplishing that goal. Although each individual dreamcatcher (unless mass produced) will have its own specific strengths, there are five general types of dreamcatchers.

It will probably not surprise you that four are based on the four elements.

AIR IS USED FOR
THOUGHT AND
COMMUNICATION.
FIRE IS USED
FOR THE SPIRIT.
WATER IS USED FOR
EMOTIONS AND
RELATIONSHIPS.
EARTH HELPS WITH
PHYSICALWELLBEING.

- **Air** is used for thought - or communication-based situations.
- **Fire** is used to support or transform spiritual or life force focused situations.
- **Water** is ideal for emotional issues or relationship situations.
- **Earth** helps with physical wellbeing and health issues.
- The final type is designed to enhance the connection and flow between earth and heaven.

This latter type is a good general-purpose dreamcatcher or one used to maintain balance or health. So if a relationship, at work or at home, is out of balance, you could hang a water-themed dreamcatcher. Once equilibrium is restored, you can switch to a connection-based dreamcatcher.

Determining the precise nature of the affect desired is often the hardest part of working

with dreamcatchers. We so often know that "something is just off" but we may not easily know exactly what that is. The next step, selecting a dreamcatcher, is not hard. As long as you keep in mind your general needs, you can follow your heart; as mentioned earlier, it is best not to think about it too much. The easiest part comes next. Simply hang the dreamcatcher in the appropriate place and let it do its job.

Remember, the dreamcatcher's functions include filtering out unhealthy and unnecessary energy and dreams, attracting useful and nourishing energy and dreams, and strengthening your connection with the spiritual plane. Depending on its components, it may also facilitate the healing and balancing of energies in an environment. Unlike regular filters (such as in fans, heaters, or air conditioners), a dreamcatcher doesn't need to be cleaned because the negative energy or bad

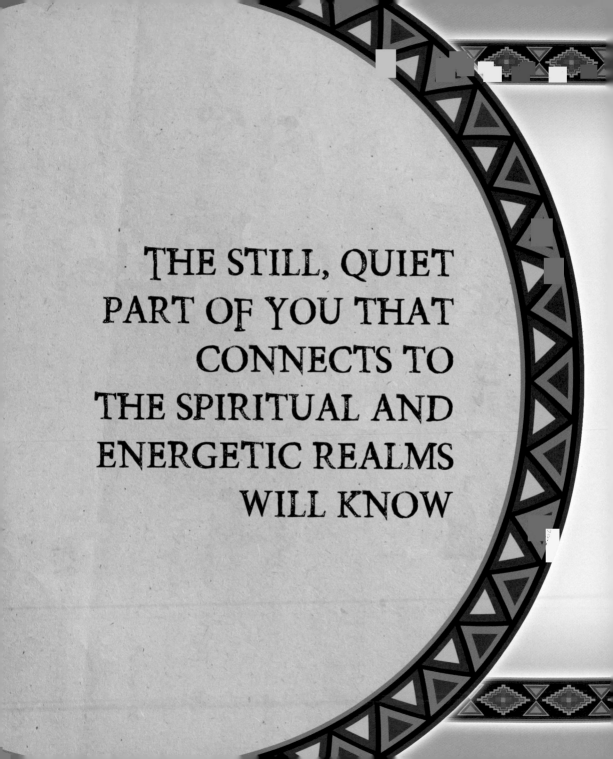

THE STILL, QUIET
PART OF YOU THAT
CONNECTS TO
THE SPIRITUAL AND
ENERGETIC REALMS
WILL KNOW

dreams captured in its web dissipate when the sun rises. The energy is broken down to its component parts and returned to the earth or the heavens where it can be reconfigured and reintegrated into the cycle of life.

You might wonder, how will I know when to take down the dreamcatcher? You won't. At least not consciously. The energies at play here are not visible and often flow beneath the awareness of your conscious mind. Therefore, you have to listen to your heart and trust your intuition. The still, quiet part of you that connects to the spiritual and energetic realms will know.

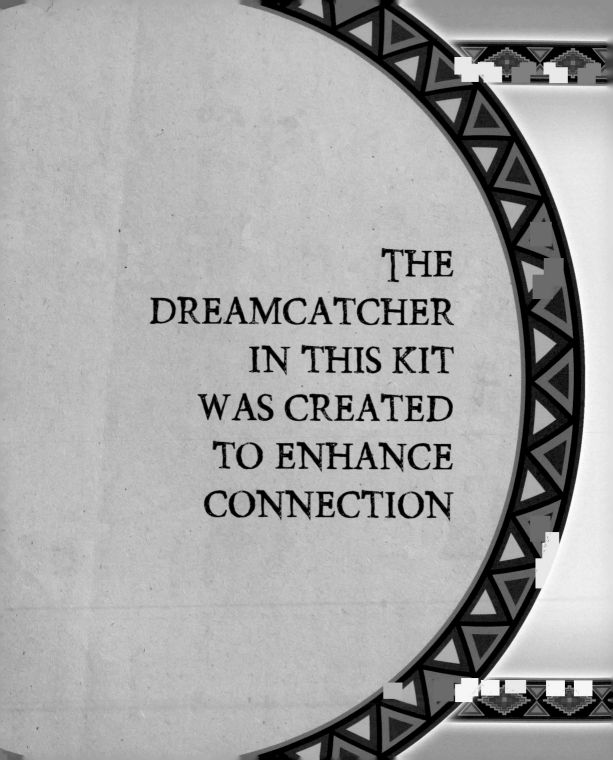

THE
DREAMCATCHER
IN THIS KIT
WAS CREATED
TO ENHANCE
CONNECTION

THIS DREAMCATCHER

The dreamcatcher in this kit was created to enhance connection, to act as a general-purpose filter to help establish and maintain balance. We wanted it to be as generally useful as possible to as many situations as possible. Consequently, we included two rings, the outer ring and the center ring, to make sure it was powerful enough for all but the direst situations. The beads are blue and black agate, to represent heaven and earth and the connection between the two. They are in a balanced pattern and on the thread to help regulate an even flow of energy. The web design is balanced both inwardly and outwardly to enhance connection. The brown rings and white feathers work together to facilitate connection and balance. This dreamcatcher will work equally well for both personal dream work and environmental stability.

HOW TO MAKE
A DREAMCATCHER

Making your own dreamcatcher can insure that it has all the components you want. Making one isn't difficult and selecting your own items, such as the circles, thread, beads, and feathers, is fun, enhances your connection to the dreamcatcher, and makes the whole experience more meaningful.

There are many tutorials and instructions online for how to make a dreamcatcher. If you cannot find someone locally to show you how, I suggest that you read as many different sets of directions as possible because it can be hard to explain how to do the weaving even though it is, in reality, not actually hard to do. Also, video tutorials (such as can be found on YouTube) are a great alternative to in-person instruction.

Furthermore, the directions for making a dreamcatcher can vary a lot, depending on how totally "do it yourself" you want to make it. For example, you can use metal rings for the inner and outer circles or you can collect willow branches to use. You can acquire and cut strips of buckskin or spin your own thread…or you can use pre-cut or pre-spun yarn or thread. Whatever level of "from scratch" you work at, just think about the simplest, most elegant way to achieve your goal and design a tool that is both attractive and effective.

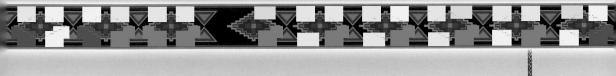

PART 3.

DREAMS

We do not completely understand what dreams are or their function. There are (and have been throughout time and cultures) many theories, of course. Here we will briefly review what are probably the most commonly accepted and popular theories about dreams, from both psychological and spiritual viewpoints.

THE PSYCHOLOGICAL NATURE OF DREAMS

Dreams are the residual processing of our day. They allow us to regulate, analyze, explain, and remember the events of the day. In reviewing these events in dream-

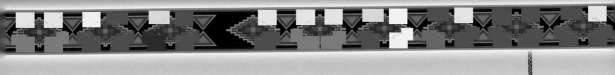

time, our mind engages in a kind of interior or mental housekeeping. Dreams, through allowing our minds to relive daily events, help solidify learning and long-term memories. In other words, they help reinforce what is most important for us to bring forward from our past experience into our future experiences. Dreams do not simply more firmly embed memories into the mind; they alter the memories in ways that make them more useful in the future. They also make judgment calls on what can be considered unnecessary. Events, facts, and experiences that are not necessary or thought of as "junk," are removed from our conscious storage area. Once the memories of daily events have been sifted through and refined, ones that are not considered "junk" are stored for future use.

Sometimes intensely disturbing experiences are stored deeply in our subconscious,

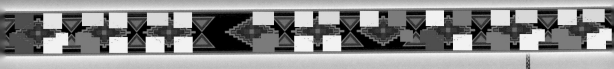

keeping our conscious mind safe from ideas that it is not prepared to accept. Over time, these ideas begin to slowly slip out, easing them into consciousness. These baby steps help prepare the conscious mind to deal with serious issues that are necessary for mental and emotional health. While these dreams may be uncomfortable, they are necessary. Remember, dreamcatchers will only stop dreams that are destructive. If a dream is difficult or upsetting but serves the purpose of restoring or maintaining mental, emotional, or spiritual health, that dream is honored and allowed to pass. To do otherwise would interfere with the natural healing process of the psyche. As a tool designed to heal and maintain balance, a dreamcatcher cannot do things that are contrary to good health.

THE SPIRITUAL NATURE OF DREAMS

Dreams connect us to the spiritual world. Or so many of us believe. Dreams have been a part of many spiritual and religious practices for, as far as we know, all of human history. In Jewish and Christian traditions, their bible tells many stories of people having both prophetic dreams and dreams about connection with God. Shamans, pagans, and native cultures do deeply meaningful work through dreams, again both prophetic and practical. Other paths have leaders or followers receiving enlightened messages through dreams. Dreams are a wonderful way to receive divine guidance and there are ways to use your dreamcatcher to enhance or increase those experiences.

First, by simply hanging a dreamcatcher over your sleeping area, you are encouraging the

77

BY SIMPLY HANGING
A DREAMCATCHER
OVER YOUR SLEEPING
AREA, YOU ARE
ENCOURAGING THE
FLOW FROM THE
SPIRITUAL WORLD
TO YOUR DREAMS.

flow from the spiritual world to your dreams. The dreamcatcher helps keep that connection clean and clear by filtering out unnecessary energy, energy that acts like static and that makes it harder to hear and see the dream. It also helps eliminate unnecessary information, or what we might call "bad" dreams or nightmares, dreams that may be drawn to us not because we need them but because we've engaged in obsessive, unhealthy thought patterns. Because like attracts like, the more we engage in negative thinking, the more we draw negative thoughts, images, and dreams to us.

This leads to a second way that dreamcatchers can help strengthen our connection to spirit, one that we can more actively participate in. So many of our negative thoughts are the by-product of our responses to expectations we put on ourselves based on society, family, friends, media, etc. If we work on

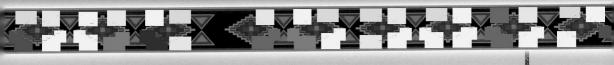

eliminating these, we make room for more positive thoughts. Also, if we focus on more positive thoughts, we give negative thoughts less power and control over our minds. Meditation is a great way to help clear the mind of unnecessary or unhealthy thoughts while inviting spiritually nourishing ideas to take root in us. Many people say that they find meditation difficult because they cannot control their thoughts or clear their minds. Luckily, you have a dreamcatcher whose job it is to filter out unnecessary, unhealthy energy, attract useful and healthy energy, and enhance your connection to the divine spirit. Meditating under a dreamcatcher is an excellent way to prepare yourself to receive spiritually important dreams and build up resistance to negative or disruptive nightmares or thoughts.

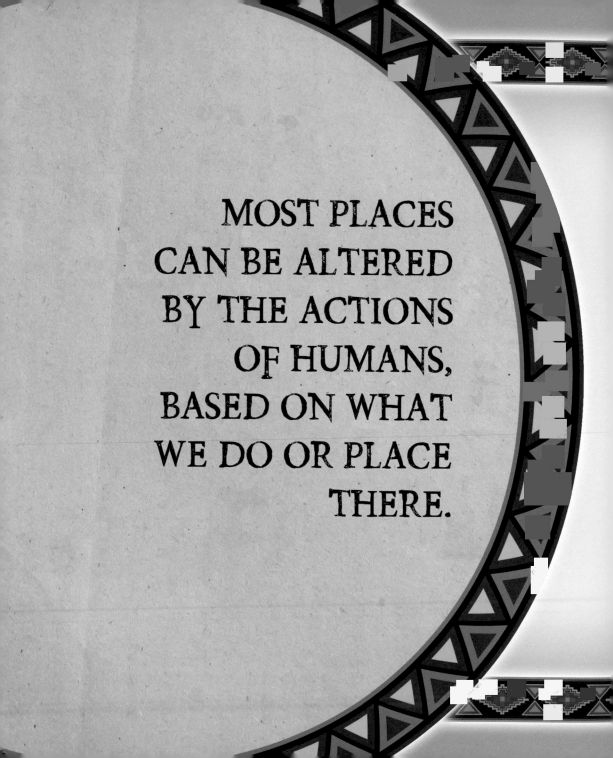

MOST PLACES
CAN BE ALTERED
BY THE ACTIONS
OF HUMANS,
BASED ON WHAT
WE DO OR PLACE
THERE.

PART 4.

ENVIRONMENT

As mentioned earlier, dreamcatchers can be hung with the intention of cleansing, transforming, and balancing the energy of any environment. Various paths, most particularly the art of feng shui, acknowledge the important connection between the material world and the flow of the invisible energetic world. Most of us have walked into rooms or buildings or outdoor spaces in nature and instantly felt the energy of a place, whether calming, chaotic, uplifting, oppressive, or any other type of energy. While it is true that some places on earth have a very particular energy that is their nature and extremely hard to change (such as Stonehenge), most places are more neutral by nature and therefore can be altered by the actions of humans, based on what we do or place there.

In order to create spaces that are most supportive of emotional, mental, and spiritual health, first you have to assess the space in terms of its energy. If you have a room or area of your house that doesn't feel right, that people remark on negatively when entering, or where arguments and misunderstandings always occur, try to determine what kind of energy prevails. Aggressive? Needy? Selfish? Controlling? Manipulative? We can think of this energy as spiritual pollution.

Then see if there is anything in the area that might be the focal point or portal or be providing support for that energy. If so, do what you can to remove or change it. Many things in the physical world can create spiritual pollution, and likewise there are things that can help maintain a healthy spiritual energy environment. Naturally, a dreamcatcher can help with this work, but if you don't assess and take care of the room and its contents, it would be like hanging up an air freshener over a pile of putrefying garbage.

First, any energy will turn "bad" if the energetic flow of the room is off. If energy cannot flow, it becomes stagnant. Like stagnant water or air, stagnant energy is heavy, oppressive, and unhealthy. The longer it hangs around, the stronger it gets. You do not have to master the art of feng shui by any means. But by using common sense, you can walk around a room and tell if the flow is natural and easy. If not, rearrange the room and possibly remove some furniture, if there is simply too much. Clutter is another thing that really affects energy flow. Having too much stuff makes life harder because you cannot easily find what you need and nothing in the space has enough room to breath. It also makes it difficult, on an energetic level, for new things to come into your life when your living space is overfull of unneeded stuff. It really is amazing how much a thorough weeding out of things changes the atmosphere in a room, and, by extension, your life. It is the simplest and most reliable magic I know.

The next easy energetic fix may not feel so easy, particularly if you don't care of housecleaning. Clutter is one thing…it is about the actual stuff. Dirt is another thing. Even if you only have three things in a room, if those things are covered in dust or dirt or spilt food or drink or whatever, if the floors are so dirty they turn your socks black, if there are cobwebs in the corners and dust bunnies under the furniture, the energy may be flowing but because, remember, like attracts like, the energy being drawn in will be in some state of decay. That's what dirt and dust are…things in various states of decay. Keeping things clean helps keep things healthy not just on an energetic level but also on mental and emotional levels. This includes things that we don't always see or think about like air filters in heating units or fans.

Once the space has been decluttered and cleaned, then you can take steps that will maintain good energetic health. We've talked about

the symbolic importance of color with dream-catchers and how color is important to humans. It can instantly change or evoke a feeling. We know that artists, restaurant designers, and advertising companies (just to name a few) understand and use color very consciously in order to create a specific response. What feeling does the color in your room invite? Rich, dark colors can be warm and cozy but if used with too heavy a hand or without any light or bright colors to balance them, they can feel oppressive and heavy. Light colors can be cool and uplifting, but if not tempered with a little warmth can feel ungrounded or icy. Use color to create the right balance for the energy you want.

Plants can definitely affect the energy of a room. Obviously sick or dying plants should be removed. Other than that, you can easily research the energetic qualities of different houseplants or even flowers (living or cut), selecting ones that will support the energy you want in your

space. Animals can also affect the energy in a space. Many doctor's offices and hospitals have fish tanks because watching fish is very relaxing. Pets, just like people, have their own individual energy that interacts with the energy of a space. Other living things can also affect the energy, such as rodents, spiders, ants, or other insects. While we understand that these beings have a right to live and are important parts of the eco-system, humans have known for millennia that sharing a living space with these creatures is not the best for us or for them.

Earlier we discussed how you might use a series of two dreamcatchers when working on trans-forming the energy of space, the first is used to either eliminate or invite specific energy, to cleanse and heal a space. Then once equilibri-um and health has been established, a different dreamcatcher is used to maintain that balance. If you kept the first dreamcatcher in the space after healing occurred, then you would simply

create an opposite kind of imbalance. Working with energy isn't difficult. It sometimes feels hard because we are not used to paying attention to the feeling of a room. Once you start looking at spaces with spiritual eyes, you will see where the problems are and will be able to, with a little knowledge and by trusting your intuition, create environments that support you and the life you want to live.

CONCLUSION

We hope that this book has been helpful and expanded your understanding of how dream-catchers work and what they are capable of. May your dreams be pleasant, inspiring, and revelatory!